IF ONLY IT WERE
Spring
EVERYDAY

IF ONLY IT WERE Spring EVERYDAY

MOHUA CHINAPPA

Srishti
PUBLISHERS & DISTRIBUTORS

Srishti Publishers & Distributors
A unit of AJR Publishing LLP
212A, Peacock Lane
Shahpur Jat, New Delhi – 110 049

editorial@srishtipublishers.com

First published by
Srishti Publishers & Distributors in 2024

Printed and bound in India

For my loving son Neel Mandana.

*May you always find poetic justice in chaos, in the debris
and feel each moment in your life with depth forever.
It is magic, after all.*

1

THE SONG OF THE ROAD

The song of the open road
Is a song
With no verses
Or magical words
It has no tempo
No lilting tune
It won't touch the heart
Or the soul anymore.

The empty by-lanes
Remind you of a sharp pain
Hammered into the conscience
Like the resounding beat
Of a broken banjo
Found in the altars of death
A pitch higher than before.

It is like a nail,
That fixed itself
On its permanent spot
With photos of the dead saints,
That sometimes
Gave hope
In the dingy lanes,
Are found no more.

This song of the road,
Reminds me
Of the choked and unheard cries
Of the trodden people,
Lost and seen no more.

Some were afoot,
Some on tracks
Some light on their step
No one heard their cries.
Now,
They are not even present
In our stories anymore.

2
MY HEART WHIMPERS

My heart whimpers,
It tears my innards
Like the little shrill cry
Of the puppy
That looks stricken,
Shivering in the heat,
Unable to bark anymore.

Its eyes
Filled with tears
At the body of its mother
Smashed on the tar
Of the big road,
All shiny and new
Obscene width,
Cutting trees
Our bellies unsatiated
With renewed vigour found now
In abundance.

The dead skin
Of the bitch
Has mixed in that black soot
The lost souls.
Just like the crossings

Invisible on the roads
To the big glitzy cars.

It is another car,
Another bus,
Another truck,
Another speeding light
No brakes found
In the little towns
Blinding the folks
With greed
Without a shred of morals,
Lying to each other some more.

The pavements are strewn
With naked bodies
Men and women
Shelter-less, hungry
Maggot, man all alike
Waiting for redemption
From a place with no name
No soul
Not owned
By anyone anymore.

3
BILKIS JAAN

The rapists
Roam free
The women cower
Hide like roaches
Their antenna shaking furiously
With the fear of death.

All it takes
Is another foot
Over their belly
Another hand
Over their mouth
They can't utter a word
Or a scream anymore.

4

THE SONG IS NOT
LILTING ANYMORE

The song is not lilting anymore
It has no tempo,
No meaningful stanzas.
Just a ghastly scale
That never reaches
The heavens above
Its sinful crescendo
Getting louder.

Screeching tyres
Screaming ears
Streaming tears
Loudly beating
The collective consciousness
Silenced now.

The valleys
The flowers
Don't bloom
On the sides anymore.
The trash
The green vomit
Of rejection lay septic
In the open sewers

Filling up
Choking the earth.

The gods weep
Satan laughs
Loud and say you little bitches
Bastards you obey me now,
All the more.

The song has no verses
Or magical words
Anymore.

5

SEPTEMBER BLUES

Surreal September
Creeps into my room
The soft sunlight
Falls on the crease of my undone bed
In full bloom
It has your presence
Mixed in nicotine and pain
It has my longing
Like jumbled-up words
Lost in an unknown terrain.
The fresh croissant fills up the room
Its butter aroma mixing with the caffeine.

6
METAMORPHOSIS

Kafka is half read
The butterfly emerges yet again
Fluttering and kissing
Every leaf and flower
Strewn around
In my garden of hope.

It stops,
Looks intently
Roams around aware
In vain.

7

ACCEPTANCE

I wonder if my manuscript would be accepted
Which will have stories of women
Who know that their bodies are their business.
It has a shelf life like the curd packets
In the supermarket shelves
That once soured won't be accepted.

Where they know that the cigarette butt stubbed
On it may fetch extra money
With the customer,
For the waterproof mascara
That mustn't run down when hurt.

The stories of the drunkard father
Who needed his fix so badly
That he stole the money
From his child's geometry box,
So he could get the peg.

The woman who put extra salt
In her ailing mother-in-law's food,
Because she was tired of cleaning
Her shit and was scared to say
The stench stayed in the agarbatti
She lit to the gods asking for
Her mother-in-law's death
And her salvation.

10

8

THE SEEKERS

I don't shun the worry lines
Found on my forehead
I am older and wiser.
The problem is for people
Who fear aging
And for the ones who have never found
Love.

I care for my loved ones
It's worrisome
What would happen?
And I cry harder
For the elderly sex workers
The terminally ill single poor women
The women forced out of their homes
Mankind in general
The ones
with no love.

I worry,
Where would they go?
On the last day of
Judgement?

9

WALK ALONE

The honest are frightened
To merge
Get lost in a crowd
Of piled-up lies.

They fear getting sucked
Into a system
That defiles their souls
Prostitutes their mind.
They fear transactions
As they always give more
And receive less.

There is light at the end of the tunnel
Among the crowds too.
Don't be afraid,
When you're losing yourself
Feeling happy, not sad
There is bravery
In knowing that only you
Get you through it all
Don't be afraid
To become one like them
Coz you will be unhappy
No matter what
In the crowd.

Walk alone,
On the ocean shore,
In the forest,
In the flaming fire
The crowd
Will fade one day,
Yet you will stay strong in
Your honesty
Because that is what will
Keep you company,
Among the debris of the
Crowd,
That cares no more.

10
LOSS IN WINNING

The mountains stood still
It watched the loyal sons
Of both the lands in blood
In death.
Lives were lost
In a war between two countries.
The rivers changed their colour
To a pink never seen before.
The blood of young soldiers
Ran its course through the melting ice
In its calm flow.
The trees swayed in horror
As the line of control was again drawn.

We won!

We were brave
What remains is the silence of the mountains
That knew the stories of a loss that is irreplaceable.

11

ON MOVEMENT AND IN CONVERSATION
WITH INANIMATE OBJECTS

I started to collect
Old things
To replace them
With new things
For my new home.
Gosh! It's a damn mess.
A home of 14 years.
Junk galore.

Old saucepans
Without the handle.
A rusty knife
That my cook promised to sharpen.
He evidently didn't use this.

Broken china
That he fixed with glue
Fix and hid it among the pile.

I began collecting
All the old things
One by one.

I looked
In the kitchen.

My coffee mug
Winked at me
What happened,
Did it happen?

I rubbed my eyes,
Blinked and again looked
At the old grey coffee mug.
The damn thing
Was now laughing at me.

I looked furtively
Found that there was no one.

I walked up to the mug
"You dare wink and smirk
I will trash you too among the old items."
"I missed you! Wait!!"
The mug spoke
The fat rotund schmuck,
The cup winked back again.

This time
I went closer,
My eyes into the mug.
Fatso!

The mug smiled and said
Look at the side,
Remember when you were careless
You carried me
You knocked me on the side of the door
And gave me this bruise?
I live with it.

Remember?

I whispered
Said, "No, I don't recall"!

Ok remember
When Dida passed away
You filled me to the brim with black coffee and wept.
Your salty tears dropped and I felt you on my arm
...you dummy you call it my handle.
It's my arm.

I have always been there for you.
Our fingers intertwined every morning
You listen to songs
Watch the butterflies in your garden.

I stay with you,
Watching you put your lip
Towards the edge of me
As you find your refuge in me.

I know you are
Pretentious many times.
You use words like
Sukoon, ishq
I have heard you
Sip your hot coffee and
When it scalded you,
You used the f-word.
I don't use words like you.

How can you forget
I am your best friend.

You carry me
Wherever you go.
So learn to clean me gently.

I have seen many a moon wane
Wax with you.

I love you.

Your broken, chipped mug.

12

I DREAM

Learning as I go along in life
Love is beautiful even in silence
Love can be cherished
In the other's absence
Love can be the strength
And as I take my steps
Over the muck
Into the clear stream of logic
I find
Love is also reasonable,
Fair and never a weakness.

13

IF HEARTS WERE
TRANSPARENT LIKE GLASS

If hearts were transparent
Like glass.
How would the world look
With their naked scars?
If heartbeats
Could be counted
Like the hands of the clock,
Would we be able to measure pain?

Would you drink
Coffee with me
If I was soaked in blood
With the crescendo of my pain beat
Like an orchestra,
Gone wildly astray?

14
TOMORROW

Oh to wake up
To the dew-kissed grass
Under my feet

To drink my morning coffee
Staring emptily at the hills
Ahead that stand
In its stoic naked strength

To be able to walk away
Without looking back at the bridges
I burnt.

To be able to carry
The seashells lying desolate
On the seashore.

Listening to the stories
Of the tiny creatures
That braved many a rough tide
Deep storms
To be washed ashore.

Today I have to wait
To sink my feet
In the wet
Receding sand

Maybe tomorrow
The shore will come to me
In all its splendour.
Today I have to wait
For tomorrow.

15
UNREQUITED

Love is fleeting
Like the clouds
Love is flowing
Like the clear stream
Love is free
But so costly
No money
Can buy love
No strength
Can mend a broken love.

If you have to love
Love knowing that in the end
There won't be love
But you must remain as beautiful
As the start of love.

16

THE DECAYING BODY
WITH A WISE MIND

I write taking a cue
From life
In the waiting rooms.

I delve back
Into the memories
Of a waiting room at the railway station.

I was 10
Ma is in her early thirties.
We had a leather suitcase,
And a water bottle,
One held all in a green coarse fabric.
I learnt to keep a sharp eye
When ma went into the loo.
She taught me these life skills.

I recall the rusty fan above
That made such a racket.
But the racket was sweeter
Than the dingy heat.
So I looked up to smile at the fan,
That never smiled back.

I was not allowed
To move.
I sat still
With ma,
Waiting
For the next train.

 Ma said
"Don't talk too much, just write all that you observe."
 I was diligent and I wrote.

I wrote
About the gorgeous hippie running away
From her home in the UK,
About the cleaner who mopped the floor
Like a chore.
Her sari above her ankles
Her hair dishevelled.

I remember
I used to lose track
Of my pen,
On paper while writing.

My mind caught the devil's dance
Of the swarming large black flies
In the chai shop at the station.
Milky tea in a kulhad.
The bookshelf selling
Cheap Hindi novels.
In that chaos
Was stardust magazine
With Rekha
Her red lipstick teasing

Yet hanging lifelessly
By a wooden clip.

I am waiting
Again today,
After many years.

The wait is outside
The dialysis room.
There are beds
Like the same train compartment.

Some dying,
Some want a little more life
Some are in complete denial.

I realise
All waiting rooms
Are alike.

We are all waiting
For something in life.
But very few are succinct
About what the ardent wait is for.

17

THE THING CALLED LIFE

Life is not easy.
It is never easy.
Ask the labourer
Whose callused
Hands bleed
Holding the bricks.
His little baby,
Wife flinch
With his gentle touch.

Ask the prostitute
On the road
Who risks her life
In a car with three men
To get her child's school fees.

Ask the little girl
In the village
Who is married
To the temple idol
The idol remains mum
When she is sent
From one rich home
To another to satisfy their lust.

Ask the drunk
Who lost his job
His mind.

Ask the ones
Languishing in jail
For no fault.

Ask the grandmothers
Of Sunderbans in Bengal
Who are selling
Their bodies
To just live.
Their homes
All swept away.

Ask the refugees
Who have lost it all
To political fights.

Life is easy for the rich
Life will remain hard for the poor.
Spirituality suits the well-heeled
Morality is for the tamed middle class
Life is never easy, ever.

18
IMMORTALITY

The Kasturi Mrig
Has no idea
About its musk.
It roams unaware
In the deep jungles,
Doing what
The herd does.

The sandal tree
Grows in its silence.
Not letting
Anyone know
About her secret fragrance.

On a full moon night,
The Mrig, the sandal tree
Look at each other.
Both sigh together,
Knowing,
Only in death is
Found their fragrance
Their immortality.

19
PERSEVERANCE

I am learning
To count my
Fingers twice
Imagining
I have
Another hand
Holding me
While I walk
Through
My testing hours.

20

SELF-LOVE IN A HARSH WORLD

I have begun
To embrace
The imperfections
In my life.

I have begun
To understand
That earning is not the cash
In my wallet,
It is the cold juice
On a hot summer noon,
My help at home
Makes for me,
Like she
Is about to quench
Her own thirst.

I have only now
Begun to love the imperfections
In my body
Face them like
"this is me... Mohua can't be Mohua without them."

All this I learnt,
While I yearned for perfection.

I became
A richer soul
As I fell, cut, bled
And walked on the sharp jagged edges
Of life with betrayal, deceit, lies and above
All loving myself in the world that I inhabit,
Which is anything but perfect.

I recently
Learnt to draw boundaries,
Recognise
Self respect.

21

THE FLIRT

The bashful flowers
Were resplendent
In their beauty.
The vain rose shook
But steadied itself
At the sunlight tried to flirt
With her half-opened buds.

22
MEET ME SOON

It is rare
To find a dew drop
Hanging only for you
To watch its fall
Into oblivion.

It's rare
To meet someone
Who can read your mind
Like a person on braille

It's rare
To find
The teardrops of your eyes
In another pair of eyes
Staring back at you telling you
....I too tear up
 In your tears.

Oh god!

That's rare.

23
FAITH

The brave lone duck
Swims on the lake
Unafraid of its depth
Or the distance
Between her and the row.

24

SHILLONG

As the serotonin tablet starts to kick
Into my body.
I feel nauseous,
Feverish
With a severely parched throat.
I find myself
Physically moving away from myself.

As I step back
To look at my life,
The years that have passed.
I recall the people
Who came and left.
The ones who left, but stayed on.

I could sense the familiarity,
Like soft rose petals on my moist skin,
All this,
That I had exchanged
For cold loneliness.

I stared back,
With dry eyes,
At the canvas
Of my life.

It resembled
A black-and-white film camera roll.

The film
That you put away
In black plastic boxes.
The film had parts in it,
That was botched
With huge stains of red.
It resembled
The colour of
Fresh blood,
Almost warm
But unflinchingly cold
In its memory.

I let my mind wander.

I can't remember
When or where was the first instance,
That I forget to feel happy.
When did I forget to smile
With all my heart?
When did I lose the track
Of the narrow meandering hill, and roads
To suddenly find me in a maze of concrete?
Concrete that was hard,
Unforgiving
To a fall
And shiny
With the sun's harsh rays on it.

I was amazed
As how far

I had courageously traversed.
I also understood
That retracing those steps is unlikely.

What was familiarity
Now for me?
I had no definitive answer.

Maybe it was the welcoming,
Known roads,
Where the sidewalk
Had railings with raindrops
Hanging like diamonds
On its edges.

I remember,
I used to run my little finger
To bring down the raindrops.
I watched it fall into its oblivion.
As the rain stopped,
At the little safe corner of the house wall
Where the evening light would fall and fade.
There the rainbow
Would often show up.
It was a dance of light and dark.

Ma would say
"The jackal just got married."
I was filled with glee
At the thought of the wedding tea party,
For which I had no invitation.

The monastery ahead
Remained hidden

Among the forests.

Those lonesome evenings,
When the Buddhist monks passed
By the house,
They always walked
In a row.
They seemed sure
Of going somewhere,
A place unknown
Yet safe.
They were solemn never unruly.
The sight of the red
And the yellow robes
Against the blue sky
Remains surreal.

The huge bamboo tree
Got greener with the rain.
I remember it swayed
In its own weight.

I remember
Tiptoeing over streams
Where the water washed every sin
Every rock in its way.

I long to go back there.

But right now
It's the serotonin
That promises to give me the lull,
That I need to reach there.

25

A PRAYER

It has been long
Since I woke up
In the arms of love.

Since I looked up
Saw the silhouette of our naked bodies
On the blades of the still fan above,
Reminding me it's spring still.

I lost count of when
I woke up happy,
Free
Sang a song
In my heart.

I covered your feet
With the corners of the sheet
So that you stay snuggled in.

I tiptoed to the bathroom
While you were asleep
I held the door gently
As I was shutting and opening
To not stir your sleep.

I loved someone intensely
And also someone
Loved me right back.

But now it's time for summer to arrive.
The sun shines
Fiercely above.
The heart to go on
Its solo journey.

My stubborn heart
Still wants to find herself
In a safe space.
She thinks
It is tough being in love again.

26
HOPE

When it seems
Impossible
When it feels
That you're lost
Remember this too shall pass
We will all wake up together
To a new dawn,
To a new beginning
So please don't lose hope
The sun will shine
The flowers will bloom
We will all come out stronger
Than ever.
Don't lose hope.

SILENCE ON THE RAILWAY TRACKS

On 8 may 2020
In Aurangabad
The air was still,
It smelt
Of an eerie dance
Of the wolves.
The labourers
Could not foresee
The doom
Walked bravely
Into the jaws of death
As they were goaded
 In search of security,
 The walk that was never
 To return ever again.
 Such was this night
 In the sleepy
 And the sleepless
 A long line of labourers
 Waiting
For their death knell.

Most of us won't understand
A hungry stomach
Or a back burnt

In the harsh noon sun.
Just like a happy person
Cannot understand a broken heart
That can never stop crying.
Many would say
Why did they stop
To sleep on the track?

The labourers
Were tired
Had trudged a long distance
Trying to escape
Death.

With the faith
Of god,
The band of the 16 labourers
Trudged the arduous path
Back home,
Withstanding the rain,
Shower the sun.
They carried
Their courage
With their little potli of rotis
A heart full of hope.

But luck
Was never their friend
Surely not on their side tonight.
They always lamented
That luck favours the rich
Strangely today
They had forgotten

That luck would not choose them again
It had already chosen
Its muse
In the prosperous
The chosen few.

It was already bad
That they had no work,
No food
The gnawing fear of death
Gripping their heart
Like the tentacles
Of a deadly snake
Each and every passing day.
They were alone in a city,
Without a name,
An identity
Or an address to call their own.

They decided to get together
Walk back home.
Back to the familiarity of family.
To their wives,
Little children, old parents.
It was the ray of hope in the dark dungeon
Of the factory shifts.

They cooked rotis
Filled little cloth bags
Cooked food
They began their journey.

Labourers are a sturdy lot.
They can withstand

More trauma than others.
They trusted the strong
Legs to take them back.
With the experience
Of life,
The faith
In their two hands
Had already given them
Food hope of a better life.

They knew all they had was their body
To rely on
And a heart full of courage
And the innate knowledge
Of the survival tricks.

The factory owners
Said, "Please carry on.
We can't help you anymore."

Businesses
Were shutting shop
The pandemic was looming larger than life.

It was a few nights
Before the full moon.
They checked
The calendar,
Called their families
To tell them
That they were leaving their job
In the city
To return back home.

The wives were frightened
But were glad
That they would be together
Even if it was in misery.

In this ruin,
Lies the story
Of Seema and Bholu.
Seema asked Bholu,
To add some achar
Between the rotis.
The dry
Sukkha rotis
Aren't easy to swallow.
Bholu promised
To do that
And he said this would soon end.
He would be back at home.

Seema fasted
That morning.
It was the wee hours,
She woke up and prayed to the sun god
Applied her sindoor
Went round the tulsi tree
To beg forgiveness
For the fights to bring Bholu safely back home.

Bholu joined the group and they began walking.
They walked
Till the back burnt
With the relentless sun
But they sang together

Kept the spirit intact.

They had not slept for days on end.
By the time dusk fell
They were losing track
The feet
Were giving away.

Sonu, the oldest among them
Said, "Let's stay close to the track
So that we don't lose
Our way."
There is quarantine
No trains will pass
This way.

They decided
To rest a bit
They lay down,
Shut their eyes
Passed away.
Deep in slumber,
They didn't hear the sound
Of the hungry wolves
The crushing
Of the train wheels
Speeding
Into the night track.

Bholu saw Seema in his dreams.
They were married
Only a few months ago.
They were expecting
Their first child.

He smiled
At the thought
Sang a tune, and slept away.

It was past midnight.
Like the train
From Pakistan,
This train was from the next village
In India.
The green flag
Was hoisted
The train took on its track.
It was pitch dark
The engine driver smiled
And started his journey
To Aurangabad ahead.

As he went blowing the whistle
In the air
Filling the air.
The train crushed bones,
Brains hearts
Under its wheels
It went on its journey
To deliver the goods ahead.

There was no sound
Because the death of the labourer
In the night, anyways is
Without much sound or mourning.

As the morning broke,
The villagers saw mutilated bodies,
Limbs,

Open boxes
With food and clothes
Strewn all around.

The army of the 16
Were gone
And there was one
Who survived
Injured and maimed.

The cries filled the air
The dogs ate the rotis
In hope of filling their hunger
Human beings stood in shame
For the abject loss of humanity
Hung their heads with pain.

I too cried
Felt the bile rise in my throat,
I put the next morsel in my mouth.
I can see the rotis on the track
I silence my mind
I tell myself that I will soon forget
Aurangabad train incident
Like I have forgotten
So many such incidents before.

Life is cheap
The poor is cheaper.
We shall continue.

But back in the village,
Seema is waiting
To see Bholu

She has no clue
That the only remains
Of her loving Bholu are
Mangled bones
Flesh
That she won't ever know
If it's her Bholu or someone else.

The track lies strewn
With rotis,
Photos of family
Screeching silence
That haunts me
Every evening
As I lie in my bed.

Train to Pakistan,
Train in Godhra,
Train in Aurangabad
All will remain
In the annals
Of history as an example
Of the abysmal loss
Of humanity
The lack of amenities
For the poor in our country.

28
WORDS

Words find me rested in the known
The unknown spaces,
In music,
Among people,
In layers of fabric
All things that are mundane
And marvellous.

Words are my muse
In sentences lies my art of expressing
What needs to be woven
Into stories.

If words are your lover
Then sentences are your music
Paragraphs are the resting spot
Exclamations are the surprises
With no full stops ever.

29

NIGHT IN A CROWDED BAR

Night
In the crowded
Weekend bar.

I can spy
With my little eye,
The pretentious conversationalist,
The bonhomie
Among the motley mix
Of the weekend revellers,
The mixed groups of friends,
The karaoke singers,
Singing
Out of tune,
The angry girlfriend
The stressed boyfriend,
The roving eyes
Of the middle-aged husband
His bored wife.
All are together,
Trying to flee
The week
Passed by
The mundane existence
Of life and living.

They are numbing
The pain, just like me,
With food
Big gulps of beer.
They have silence
In the soul and no smiles
To give each other,
Yet smile
For the stranger,
They have not met yet.
They also stare
Around lifelessly
At the people,
Who disinterest them.
Most are disintegrated,
Dismembered fragmented
United in the quest for an escape.

I stand
In the queue
Outside
The girl's washroom.
Some of them giggle,
Some laugh loud,
Some are standing alone,
Waiting for their turn
To take a piss at life.

In all of this
Is also the reeking stench
Of a failed escape.
It smells

Of a mixture of burnt nicotine,
Toxic urea that is being forced
To be freshened
By the carbon dioxide.

Yet it fails
To camouflage
The stink in spite
Of the naphthalene balls
Strewn
Around the toilet bowl.
The staggering drunkards
Miss the dirt
But don't forget
To take a look
At themselves
In the lit-up mirror
That laughs lies with them.

Each of them,
Like me,
Are seeking solace
From the grind of the shared realities.
The alcohol-
Infused breath
Is all-pervading
With the stale thoughts
Of coping
With life tomorrow,
The day after.

From the dark,
Unlit corner

Of the carpet
Stares a sly cockroach,
With long antennas
Trying to get a bit of its unwanted space
In this drunken stupor.
The Moon
Above shines
In its pristine glory,
Giving light to its being.

It is another weekend
In a city
Where dreams
Are broken and built,
Hearts are shattered
Hope is in the bottle
Music for those few hours
Of borrowed happiness.

There are the tired cleaners
On the side,
Waiting for the revellers
To leave,
So that the carpets
Are cleaned,
The tables are wiped,
The bottles are picked.

The lucky cockroach
Escapes its death
The bar is ready
For another evening,
Another day

In the city
Where the lights
Are bright
The souls are dim
With darkness.

30
ROAD-LOVE SONG

It began
As a promise!

A sign
That this memory
Would last
Forever.
The smell
Was abounding
In the swaying
Palm trees
The hungry
Parched land
The sounds
Came like a fury
From the heavens above.

Then it began
Its slow downpour
First in large drops
Over my windshield
Then the curves
The bends on the hills
Bathing
In its first shower

Love and purity from above.

I touched
A drop on my finger
Felt it
Wet my soul
He drove on
A smile playing on his lips
The radio played our favourite song.

It was midnight
The owls
Screamed
The clouds roared.

It was lashing rains
In fury and passion
The parched earth
Soaked in the wetness
From the heavens above
Like a lost lover
Found the self again
In glory
In serenity.

The windshield was covered
In sheets of water
It poured
Into its infinity
In the darkness
Thunderstorm appeared from above
I knew
This was what the gods
Decided from above.

I held his arm
He rested
In the knowledge
Of my touch
Just like the familiarity
Of the known
Just like the parched earth
The torrential rains
From above.

I left behind
Towns, lanes
Found me again
In the promise
Of us together.

This moment
Was meant to be
Today
Was for tomorrow
A promise
Of a lifetime memory
The rain,
The roads,
The song.

You & I
With our broken promises
The past held together
By the rains
We had today
For tomorrow
And after.

31

WOULDN'T YOU WISH?

This is an ode to love
That I love to love
My wish
To never ever stop loving.

Wouldn't you wish?
Wouldn't you wish that
The brightest stars
Melt on our bodies
We both held our hands,
Fingers entwined
In each other
We catch the glow
Of the shining stardust
Between our fingers.

We would be on the bed
The glass roof above
Listen to the first drop of rain
Blink our eyes
Till the rain
Would pound
Above our heads
Leave flowers
And leaves hanging

And slowly cascade
Down the glass
Like lost painful
Memories of the past.
Wouldn't you wish?

Don't you wish
We would sit by the bonfire
Drink hot chocolate
Look at the town ahead
As the splinters of fire
Would break the monotony
Of the horizon ahead.

I do want to wake up
With you
In to the cold air
On my nose
Cheeks
As I hold you
Like life itself.
All the pain melting
Away in that moment
As we find
Our destiny
Entwined
The stars melting on our bodies.

Right now,
If I had wings
You had wings too
We would fly away
To the mountains

That has a home
With our address

We would call it Firdaus.

32
MEMORIES

In the cold winter
Drizzle of a rainy day,
I nudge nostalgia
With gusto
Pouring with abundance
Oozing it into my very being.

This is my favourite indulgence,
It needs no internet connection.
I can play
My own life,
In my heart
Get glassy-eyed,
Like a dope fix
That just overwhelms
My senses.

It is the memory of a loss
Of a good friendship,
The goodbye
I didn't say
With gratitude,
The lost lovers
The lone passerby
Who shook me
With their sheer presence.

To trip with memories,
It sometimes just takes
The divinity
Of a lone raindrop
On the mossy floor
Of loss.
I recall
The truck ride
From Shillong in 1984
At 2.00 am
Our little belongings
In a leather
And metal trunk
To Delhi
Via Assam
To board my train
To freedom.

It was the time of insurgency
The army wanted to help
Rekha and her little girl
Escape,
Being lit
As they slept
In their warm room.

When I watch
A cold drizzling winter rain,
I allow
That cold to enter my bones
Relive that
Moment of nostalgia.
That great escape.

I feel a delicious thrill
To recall those moments of death
And life.
I realise
There is no joy
In living life,
Without being ransacked
Of your best emotions,
It teaches us to be grateful
For a free life, as human beings.

Time and again,
I delve deep
To feel the same gripping fear,
The marching of the army boots
Over my head
The running of the fox-like tribals
Into the bamboo marshes ahead.

The suffocation
When Rekha would cover my mouth,
So that the sound of my heavy fearful breath
Does not give away
The insecurity
Behind the four walls,
We called home.

The photos of the smiling plastic god
As hope in hopelessness.

Nostalgia can be pretty ugly.
Ugly ones last longer.

However hard I try
To forget,
The eyes remain to stare
Through the slit of the window
To check how many he could kill,
To take revenge.
This too is nostalgia
Of a different kind,
But nostalgia whatsoever.

33
ELUSIVE

Love is momentary
It is as fleeting
As the clouds
Over the azure skies.
It lasts
For a while.
Enjoy
Those moments
It's not meant to last forever
When it comes to an end
When you feel down
With the closure
Just let it pass
Like the calm clouds.
Indulge in yourself
And some lonesome time.
Love will come again
It will also leave again
In this moment of despair
Love yourself fiercely
Over and over again.

34
COVID

The agony
Of 2020 has come full circle.
It is the time of humility,
An acknowledgement
Of the fragility of life,
That we think we own.

This year
We were forced to address
The felling of large trees
To broaden roads,
That had no cars.
This disruption of nature,
We normally address
Only for a few seconds
And in the same breath,
We curse the narrow roads
In burgeoning cities,
Bursting at its seams.
We remain confused
What we seek
Desire.

Mindless material consumption,
We choke in its addiction

More and more.
Yet we continue blinded
For the next dopamine fix.

It takes me back to the scene
In Mahabharat, where Kunti
Is blindfolded
To watch her sons
Disrobe Draupadi,
All along Dhritarashtra
Remains blind
To the heinous act.

To me,
We are watching
The same scene being played out
In a modern setting,
With greed, anger,
Foolishness
Of
Thinking,
Money can buy anything.

Domestic violence
Is on the rise
As men lose their jobs
Are forced to sit at home.

First time they are part
With the harassed wife.
A setup of two rooms
With large families,
Sometimes one room,
Limiting personal space,

The ailing parents,
The child's rising loan

For a digitised education system.

Some have perished
With the breathlessness of Covid 19
Some stoically survived the pandemic.

We can only hope that life will resume
Where the blindfold for injustice falls off,
Gardens and parks
Have little children
Playing and this ghastly sight
Of masked men and women
Comes to an end.

The debauchery of nature
Is a big cost to pay, human beings.
This pandemic
Also teaches us to live
With melancholy
As a constant companion,
With the fear
Of death lurking
In every human interaction.
This is Gotham revisited.

With hope,
I shut
My eyes,
I dream
Of a fresh spring,
Pretty

Summer flowers,
Hot broths
In warm homes
During winters.
A free 2021.

35
BELONGING

The mind is fluid
Its innate
Need is to flow
Like the river.

And just like the river
It has to carve
Its own path.

This is not given
Or found easily.

Like the river,
The mind
Over time learns
To gurgle,
Leap gush over
The rough rocks,
Bitterness.

With all its might
It tries to follow the path.

Sometimes it is unable
To flow serene, calm.

But it does not give up.

Drop by drop
It finds its way
Between
The dark strong
Jagged edges.

And through the crevice,
It begins to slowly flow.

Always
Determined to reach
The clearer
Surer path into the belly of the ocean.

Like the child
Into the lap
Of the mother.

The mind too
Must go
Through the dark times,
Rough edges
To find
A clearer path.

36

JUST ONCE AGAIN

Just once again
I could try
To mend
The broken parts
Of my heart.
Parts that
Have not seen
Any sunlight.
I could try
To tap
Into my own divinity.

The mountains
Beckon me,
It tells me
I am here
To watch you.
Iron out
The creases
Of your heart,
Unfold the folded corners
That lie desolate.
In that corner
You refuse
To look at

If the frozen emotions
Could melt
Under this spell of nature.

The lost emotions
Rigid as stone,
If only this sunlight
Could melt those corners
That have been comfortable
Familiar
With the all-pervading darkness.

Yes, I promise
My love
I will try hard
My love
To make friends
With the emotions
Of my mad mind
That runs amok
Telling me
It got over
You don't even recall
When
Or maybe
It never did.

It just needs
The soft sun rays again,
Just once again.

37

TO ALL THE DAUGHTERS OF TOMORROW

You own your own body
Mind
Moral standards
Own yourself like nobody
Ever can
Or should.

Anyone
Who wishes
To own you
Has to learn
To own
Your soul
Spirit
But before
Any of that
He has to fucking own himself
In his totality
Honesty
Freedom
Morality.

Also remember
The immoral

Who wear their immorality
Shamelessly
On their sleeves are the
Most moral
Of them all.

38
END OF A DREAM

Dreams
Are meant to be a reminder
Of waking up
To realise dreams
Can become a reality
With the right conviction
And passion.
I daydream all the time.
I dream of a home
In the hills in Himachal Pradesh.
I dream of writing
Alongside the painter is painting on the frame...
His torso, bare and beautiful.

He is graying, with wisdom
Has Knowledge abound.

Music is playing
While coffee is brewing.
All Turkish rugs were thrown in
I am busy producing award-winning writing
I think daydreaming helps
In being happy.

39

I MET ELENA BY THE BRIDGE

I met Elena by the bridge
Of the golden
River Arno.

Elena was dressed like a queen
Wearing an emerald green silk dress
Red lipstick on her thin lips
All in place
Not a bleed anywhere.

We smiled
Exchanged
Our female
Camaraderie

She offered to click
My photo
And I offered to do the same.

Elena's smile couldn't hide the tears behind her eyes
A life lived in the promise
Of love in return.

Her wrinkles were shining
Like stardust on her kind face

Her deep neckline
Couldn't care to hide
The children
She had birthed
And the breasts
Now dry
And unused.

Finally Elena
Looked like she was home
All in herself
A totality
In herself.

She stood in solitude
By the bridge.

She confided to me
She always wanted to come
Here
This exact spot
To watch
The setting sun
On the magical
River Arno.

But she wasn't free
Free from accountability
From judgement.

Free
From the life
That wasn't
The way

It turned out
To be.

The sun was now a dark orange
The river turned red
In its belly
Reflecting the summer sun
Like our bleeding uterus
And
Our unfulfilled promises.

Arno glowed,
Surreal and womanly.

Elena said goodbye
To me
As she soaked
In the beauty
Of the place
Meant for romantics
For seekers
Like she
And
Me.

Couples kissed
Made promises
To keep.
Arno flowed
Knowing
The course shall run,
Of age
Of loss
Of life.

Many Elenas
Many Mohuas
Will stand
In awe
With hope
Dashed
Some
Resurrected.

Yet Arno will continue
To flow,
Waiting
To meet
The ocean.
Her lover
Her resting place
All
No longer in vain
In her golden glow.

40
AGEING

I am 76 years old
Ageing
Wrinkled
Dry
Flooding.

I am
Oscillating between Extreme
Weather conditions
I am tired
But
Not yet weary.

Am I free?
At 76, I ask myself.

I am confused
Between my
Freedom
And
My choices.

My freedom
Says

I can choose
But
My choice
Is never
Free.

I have been soaked
In the blood
Of my children.

The blades of grass
Sharp and bleeding
A clammy wetness
Blanketed into my soil.

Which is
My body
Unseen
Unheard
Yet
Worshipped
In obscene glory.

The women
Were paraded
Nude
Over my bosom.

Every drop of her sweat
Every inch of her fear
From her defiled body
Burns into
The pit of my stomach
Like the crazy

Burning crops of a tempestuous summer
Where vegetation withers
In shame
And
In disgust.

I roar
In thunder
I weep
In rain
Drowning villages,
Towns and cities.

Am I free
At 76 years of age?
Is my question writ large.
Yet
Unread
And
Unseen.

I can tell you
That each drop of her sweat
Each sigh from her heart
Will bring mankind
More doom,
But I have no one
Who
Listens
To me.

Even after 76 years,
I am not yet
Free.

She confided in me
That
She can't anger
Anyone
His anger
Will be avenged
By rape
By sodomy
Or
By acid
To burn
Her body
Face
Genitals
Hair
And
Whatsoever
He can see.

She needs to learn a lesson
As a woman
Even
After 76 years.
That she
Isn't free

For political
And
Historical reasons
Her body
Is the bloodied
Battleground.

Even at 76 years
Like me
She too
Is not yet free

She said
I will be paraded
Naked
Groped
Like the
Brutes
In the arena
Will be
My husband
My brother
My friends
My neighbours
As my mother
And I
Will be raped
In public view.

The crowd will
Jeer and clap

As my body
Will be mutilated
Severed.

So I tell you,
I am 76 years old
Not yet free.
But

I am not giving up
As my anger
Is awakened
My hope
Is born

Once again.
Like droplets of rain
My 76 years
Whispered to me,
Don't give up.
We will
Together
Someday
Maybe one day
Be free.